my first
Puzzle
BOOK

ARCTURUS

ARCTURUS

This edition published in 2019 by Arcturus Publishing Limited
26/27 Bickels Yard, 151–153 Bermondsey Street,
London SE1 3HA

ISBN: 978-1-78950-316-6
CH007017NT

Illustrator: Amanda Enright
Designer: Trudi Webb
Cover designer: Ms Mousepenny
Writer: Lisa Regan
Editors: Joe Harris and Frances Webb

Supplier 33, Date 0519, Print run 8587

Printed in China

Whoops!

Each of the jester's juggling balls has a matching pair. What type of ball has he dropped?

Hungry Mice

How many apples are here?
Are there enough for each
mouse to have one?

Sport the Difference

Look at these sporty kids.

Find six differences between the two pictures.

Polly the Painter

s	y	e	l	l	o	w	y
b	t	r	a	c	i	p	e
l	p	i	n	k	m	g	e
u	b	m	h	v	l	r	u
e	s	b	w	s	l	e	w
r	o	o	f	c	d	e	q
c	t	r	e	d	m	n	f
z	g	u	p	n	x	c	k

YELLOW

PINK

BLUE   GREEN   RED

Can you find all of Polly's paints hidden in the grid? Look for the words going up and down or from side to side.

Hidden Treasure

Prue's dad has hidden his most precious pirate treasure in two identical chests. Help her find the two that match.

Picnic Puzzler

Which picnic blanket has the most spots?
Help Ben and Lottie find it.

8

Feeling Proud

Use pens, pencils, and crayons to decorate this peacock's beautiful tail.

Monster Mash-up

Join the monster fun and see if you can find a monster like the one in the picture frame.

Underwater Art

Join the dots in the correct order to finish the picture.

Made to Match

12

Modern Art

This isn't just a work of art, it's also a maze! Find a way along the yellow lines, from start to finish.

START

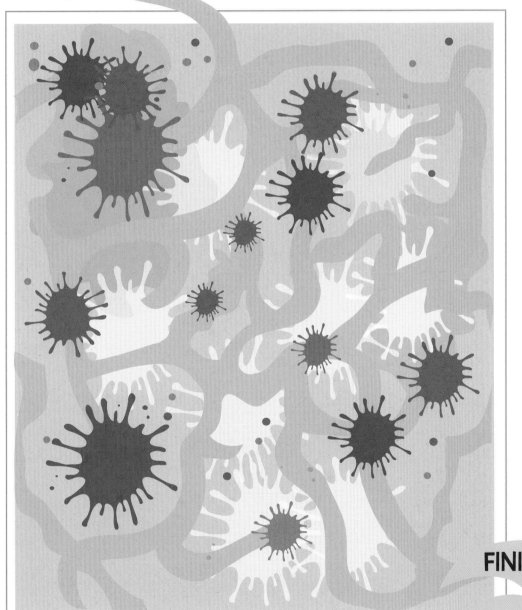

FINISH

Thirsty Work

Mickey Monkey wants to water his flowers. Which hose should he turn on?

a b c d

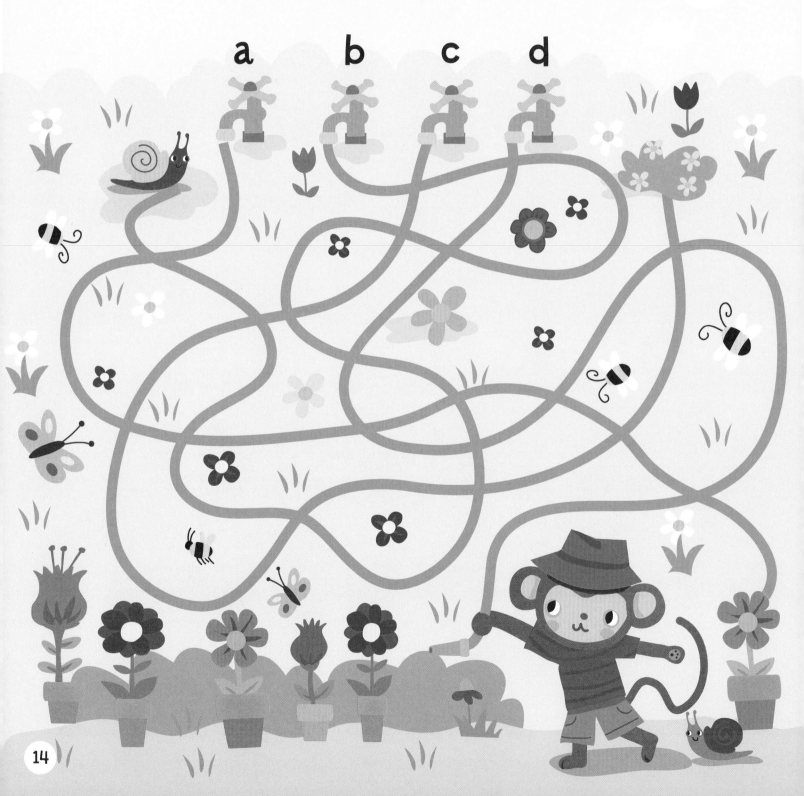

Work of Art

What has Issy drawn? Join the dots in the correct order to find out, and then finish it with your crayons.

Percy's Potion

It is in a round bottle.
It has bubbles in it.
It isn't blue.

Daisy Chain

Fifi the fairy is making a necklace. Which flower should she add next to finish the pattern?

Clown Around

Help Jimmy the clown collect three green juggling balls on his way to the Big Top.

Monster Munch

Lenny loves cupcakes and Benny loves donuts! Which monster can eat the most treats?

Playground Ride

Which of the shadow shapes matches the picture of Annie at the playground?

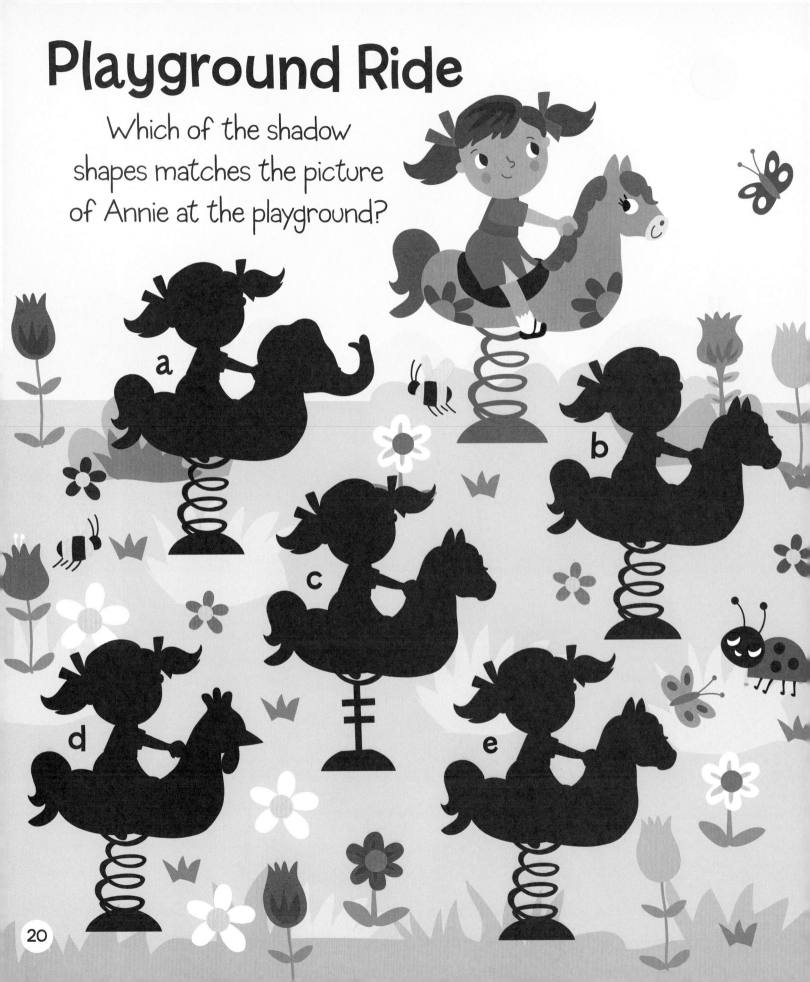

A Treat to Eat

Join the dots to reveal a tasty treat! Add some toppings to make it look extra yummy.

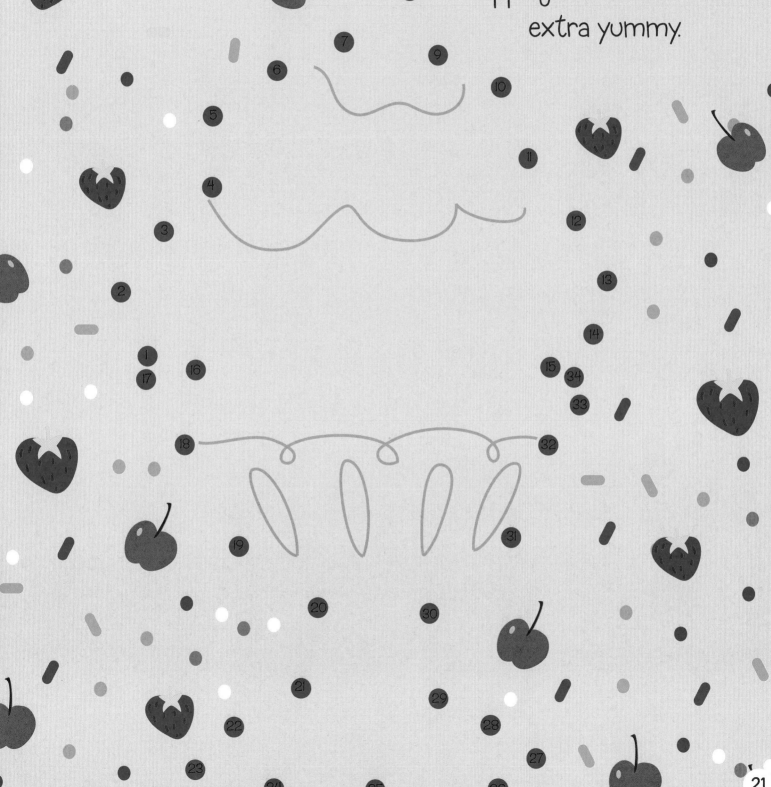

Animal Mad!

Jessica loves all sorts of animals! Find the ones she likes best hidden in this grid.

```
l i z a r d h c
p r f n l f m a
a r d o g i o p
r a b b i t u a
f k m d o n s r
i h a m s t e r
s s e c a t s o
h a b b i y g t
```

cat

dog

mouse

hamster

rabbit

parrot

lizard

fish

Answers

Page 3:
Whoops!
The jester has dropped a green ball with yellow squiggles.

Page 4:
Hungry Mice
There are 10 mice and 10 apples, so there's enough for one each!

Page 5:
Sport the Difference

Page 6:
Polly the Painter

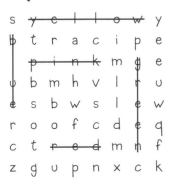

Page 7:
Hidden Treasure

Page 8:
Picnic Puzzler
Blanket c

Page 10:
Monster Mash-up

Page 11:
Underwater Art

Page 12:
Made to Match

Page 13:
Modern Art

Page 14:

Thirsty Work

Hose d

Page 15:

Work of Art

Page 16:

Percy's Potion

Page 17:

Daisy Chain

Flower a

Page 18:

Clown Around

Page 19:

Monster Munch

Benny can eat the most treats; Lenny can eat 6 cupcakes and Benny can eat 9 donuts.

Page 20:

Playground Ride

Shadow e

Page 21:

A Treat to Eat

Page 22:

Animal Mad!

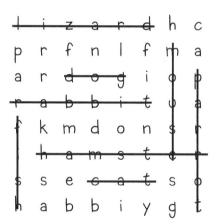